MW00933439

DAILY AFFIRMATIONS

365 Days of Powerful and
Transformative Affirmations to
Start Your Day

Aiden Stillwater

Publishing Company: BlueTree Publishing House

Publishing Company Info: Chandler, Arizona-
www.bluetreepublishinghouse.com

Aiden Stillwater

TABLE OF CONTENTS

INTRODUCTION

Welcome to Daily Affirmations: 365 Days of Powerful and Transformative Affirmations to Start Your Day - your daily companion on a transformative journey towards a brighter and more fulfilling life. If you've picked up this book, chances are you're looking for a way to infuse more positivity, confidence, and joy into your days. Whether you're a seasoned practitioner of affirmations or just beginning to explore their potential, you've arrived at the perfect starting point.

Imagine starting your day with a seed of positivity and a powerful thought that can shape your entire day's outlook. That's what an affirmation is - a positive statement that can help you challenge and overcome self-sabotaging and negative thoughts. When you repeat them often and believe in them, you can start to make positive changes. Studies say that when repeated for 4-5 minutes each day, the mind begins to reshape how you think and feel about yourself. Do you have 4-5 minutes to spare... maybe not, but you do shower, brush your teeth, make your morning cup of coffee, or even use the restroom in the morning. Use this time to start your affirmations without having to add something that takes more time out of your day.

Want some more great news? This isn't just a concept; science backs the power of affirmations. Psychologists and neuroscientists have uncovered that our thoughts can shape our reality. Sounds like magic? It's a blend of mindset, practice, and persistence.

In this book, you will embark on a 365-day journey through carefully curated affirmations designed to resonate with various aspects of your life. From embracing self-love to nurturing relationships, unlocking creativity, and finding joy in the smallest things - there's an affirmation for every part of your soul.

Each day's affirmation comes with a brief explanation to deepen your understanding and connection with the words you'll be saying to yourself. You'll be guided through stories, facts, questions, and metaphors that ignite your thought process. You've picked this book up for a purpose, and that purpose can be deeply personal, which is why this book will help you on your journey by:

- **Starting Fresh With Positivity Every Day**: It's a new opportunity to set a positive intention. Whether it's a new year, new month, or just a new day, each page you turn to is a step towards a brighter you.

- **Practical and Easy**: These affirmations are designed to be simple yet impactful. You can easily integrate them into your daily routine.

- **Support and Encouragement**: Consider this book a friendly guide, always there to uplift you, especially on the days when you might need it most.

- **You're Not Alone**: Join the Good Vibes Tribe of readers who are on this same path, a community cheering you on.

So, are you ready to begin?

If you're reading this, you've already taken the first courageous step towards positive transformation. With each affirmation, you'll be planting the seeds of change that can flourish into a garden of joy, confidence, and abundance.

So why wait? Turn the page, and let's begin this beautiful journey together. Your path to a more positive and fulfilling life starts here and now. Here's to embracing the high vibe of living and waking up with positivity every single day!

CHAPTER 1:
Embracing Self-Love

As the first rays of sunlight peek through your curtains, signaling the start of a brand new day, there's an innate sense of hope and possibility. Each morning presents a fresh canvas, waiting to be painted with the colors of our choices, emotions, and actions. What if you could start your day not with doubts or anxieties but with self-love and acceptance? Imagine greeting your reflection with a smile, deeply feeling that you are enough just as you are. This isn't just wishful thinking; it's a reality waiting to be unlocked.

"To love oneself is the beginning of a lifelong romance," Oscar Wilde once said. While the world might continuously push ideals, expectations, and judgments upon us, the journey of self-love starts by silencing these external noises and tuning into our own unique frequency. It's about acknowledging our flaws, celebrating our strengths, and being our own biggest cheerleader.

The road to self-love isn't always straightforward. There might be days when self-doubt tries to overshadow your confidence. But remember, like any other relationship, the one you share with yourself also requires effort, patience, and understanding. And this chapter, "Embracing Self-Love," is the first step in that beautiful journey.

Over the next 28 days, you'll encounter affirmations designed to anchor you in self-compassion and acceptance. They will serve as daily reminders of your worth, nudging you to treat yourself with the same kindness and respect you'd offer to a dear friend.

So, as you open this chapter, take a deep breath and allow yourself a moment of introspection. Reflect upon all the times you've been your harshest critic, vowing now to replace those self-deprecating thoughts with love and acceptance. Embrace these affirmations wholeheartedly, for they are the seeds of self-love that you'll be sowing into the soil of your soul.

Prepare yourself for this transformative journey. With each affirmation, you're not just reading words but weaving a protective armor of love, shielding yourself from doubts and negativity. So, let's embark on this intimate journey of self-discovery, cherishing the beauty of being unapologetically you. 🌷💝

"Your task is not to seek for love, but merely to seek and find all the barriers within yourself that you have built against it." - Rumi.

As you move forward, remember that this book isn't just a reading exercise; it's a commitment to yourself. A promise that each day, come what may, you will prioritize self-love. And as you turn the page, the world of positive affirmations awaits to guide you towards a deeper connection with the most important person in your life: **You.**

1. **Affirmation:** I am worthy of love and respect.

   Recognizing your inherent worth fosters self-respect, enabling you to set healthy boundaries and demand the love and respect you deserve.

2. **Affirmation:** I love and accept myself unconditionally.

   This affirmation helps to lay the groundwork for self-compassion, allowing you to embrace yourself fully without judgment or criticism.

3. **Affirmation:** My imperfections make me unique and special.

   This affirmation celebrates your individuality, encouraging you to embrace your imperfections as a vital part of who you are.

4. **Affirmation:** I am kind and gentle with myself.

   Practicing kindness towards yourself sets a positive tone for your overall well-being and helps you navigate life's challenges with grace.

5. **Affirmation:** I trust myself and my instincts.

   Trusting yourself strengthens your decision-making abilities and helps you navigate life's uncertainties with confidence.

6. **Affirmation:** I am enough, just as I am.

   Accepting yourself as enough without needing to prove anything to others fosters self-contentment and inner peace.

7. **Affirmation:** I am proud of myself and my achievements.

   Taking pride in your accomplishments, big or small, fuels your self-confidence and motivates you to strive for more.

Congratulations! You have completed your first week. This is no small step in the journey and process of change. Everyone has to start somewhere, and you should feel a sense of pride and accomplishment in sticking with it for your first week.

To be honest, this is the easy part. The first week is where most of us get to and then look around and say, I don't feel any different; this isn't working. I should just give up and stop.

FALSE!!

You may not be feeling different just yet, but you have just begun the journey of self-love and positivity. To put it in mathematical terms, you are only 1.9% complete on your year-long journey.

How about a bit of science? According to a recent study, the old myths have been debunked. They used to say it took 21 days to form a habit, which was sadly…wrong. Then they said it takes about 2 months for a new habit to form, and once again, they were found to be wrong. A new study suggests that a new habit can take between 4-7 months to stick. What does this mean for you? Keep up the great work you have begun.

You are laying the foundation for a new you, but the foundation is still incomplete; it is not concrete yet, and we still have work to do in order to have a solid foundation to build on. See you tomorrow as we continue your transformative journey!

1. **Affirmation:** I embrace my emotions without judgment.

   Recognizing and accepting your emotions without judgment builds emotional intelligence and supports mental well-being.

2. **Affirmation:** I honor my body and treat it with care.

   Respecting and caring for your body promotes physical health and a positive body image.

3. **Affirmation:** I am resilient and can handle life's ups and downs.

   This affirmation helps build resilience and a positive outlook, no matter what life throws your way.

4. **Affirmation:** My thoughts and opinions are valuable.

   Recognizing the value of your thoughts and opinions fosters self-assurance and promotes open and authentic communication.

5. **Affirmation:** I am free from self-doubt and fully believe in myself.

   Casting aside self-doubt empowers you to pursue your dreams and trust in your abilities.

6. **Affirmation:** I forgive myself for past mistakes and learn from them.

   Self-forgiveness is essential for personal growth, enabling you to learn from your mistakes and move forward without carrying unnecessary burdens.

7. **Affirmation:** I attract positive energy and love.

   Emphasizing positivity and love helps create an uplifting environment that nurtures both yourself and your relationships.

8. **Affirmation:** I am patient with myself and my progress.

   Practicing patience with yourself fosters a gentle approach to personal development, recognizing that growth takes time.

9. **Affirmation:** My self-worth is not determined by others.

   Understanding that your worth isn't tied to others' opinions allows you to stay true to yourself and your values.

10. **Affirmation:** I celebrate myself and my journey.

    Celebrating your own journey acknowledges the effort and progress you've made, boosting self-appreciation.

11. **Affirmation:** I choose positive thoughts that nurture my soul.

    Selecting uplifting and nurturing thoughts helps build a positive inner dialogue, which shapes your overall mindset.

12. **Affirmation:** I am grateful for who I am and who I am becoming.

    Gratitude for yourself fosters a positive outlook, recognizing the growth and potential within you.

13. **Affirmation:** I let go of negative self-talk and embrace positivity.

    Releasing negative self-talk enables you to replace it with supportive and encouraging thoughts, promoting self-love.

14. **Affirmation:** I am at peace with my past and excited for my future.

    Accepting your past and looking forward to the future fosters a positive outlook and encourages continued growth.

15. **Affirmation:** I embrace self-care as a vital part of my well-being.

    Recognizing self-care as essential empowers you to prioritize your needs and maintain a balanced life.

16. **Affirmation:** I am confident in my decisions and choices.

    Confidence in your decisions supports personal autonomy and strengthens your sense of self.

17. **Affirmation:** I radiate love, kindness, and understanding.

    Radiating love and kindness towards yourself and others fosters a loving and compassionate environment.

18. **Affirmation:** I am in control of my feelings and thoughts.

    Taking control of your thoughts and feelings empowers you to choose positivity and constructive self-talk.

19. **Affirmation:** I am grateful for my unique qualities.

    Appreciating your unique qualities celebrates your individuality and boosts your self-esteem.

20. **Affirmation:** I am open to growth and personal development.

    Embracing personal growth as a continuous journey fosters an open mindset, ready to evolve and thrive.

21. **Affirmation:** I trust the journey, knowing I am on the right path.

    Trusting in your journey and path builds confidence in your choices and instills a sense of purpose and direction.

These affirmations for embracing self-love are designed to nurture a compassionate and loving relationship with oneself. By integrating these positive affirmations into daily practice, readers can cultivate a more positive self-image and learn to appreciate and love themselves in a deeper and more fulfilling way.

4-Week Milestone Celebration: "Embrace Your Growth" ❦

Congratulations! You've reached a significant milestone in your journey towards cultivating a more positive mindset. These past 4 weeks have been about dedication, growth, and self-discovery. Take a moment to reflect on how far you've come and the changes you've noticed in your mindset, behavior, and overall feelings.

Activities to Celebrate Your 4-Week Milestone:

1. **Reflection Journal**: Dedicate 15 minutes to journal about the most impactful affirmations from the past month. How have they changed your perspective? What shifts have you noticed in your daily life?

2. **Gratitude Jar**: Create a gratitude jar. Write down 10 things you're grateful for from the past month and place them in the jar. Whenever you need a pick-me-up in the future, pull out a gratitude note to remind yourself of the positives in your life.

3. **Share Your Journey**: Talk to a close friend or family member about your experiences over the past 4 weeks. Sharing your progress not only cements your commitment but also inspires others.

4. **Create Your Affirmation Art**: Choose your favorite affirmation from the past month and create a piece of artwork or craft that represents it. This could be a painting, a doodle, or even a decorative note you can stick to your mirror.

5. **Mindful Meditation**: Spend 10 minutes in a quiet meditation reflecting on your growth. Focus on your breath and visualize a

tree, imagining its roots going deep into the ground, representing your growing foundation of positivity.

6. **Celebrate with a Treat**: Reward yourself with something you love, be it your favorite meal, a spa day, or even just a leisurely walk in the park. You've earned it!

Inspirational Quote:

"Growth is never by mere chance; it is the result of forces working together." - James Cash Penney.

Remember, the journey towards positivity and self-improvement is ongoing. Celebrate every milestone, no matter how small, and always look forward to the infinite possibilities that lie ahead. Continue to embrace the power of affirmations and let them guide you towards an even brighter future. 🌀 🎉

CHAPTER 2:
Cultivating Gratitude

Did you know that practicing gratitude can actually rewire your brain? According to neuroscientists, expressing thankfulness consistently can stimulate the brain to produce feel-good hormones, leading to an improved mood, better sleep, and even stronger immune systems.

We live in an era of instant gratification. From same-day deliveries to binge-watching TV series, everything seems to be available at our fingertips, which often makes us forget the importance of patience and the joy of anticipation. In many ways, this modern age has detached us from feeling genuinely grateful for the things we have, the experiences we undergo, and the people we encounter. The phrase "Count your blessings" is sometimes whispered amidst the cacophony of our busy lives, but seldom heeded.

Gratitude, in its simplest form, is the act of recognizing and appreciating the good in life. It's that moment of pause when you take in a breathtaking sunset, the quiet "thank you" to the universe when something goes right, or the deep appreciation you feel for loved ones who stand by you. It's the counterbalance to the stresses and strains of everyday urban living.

So, why focus on gratitude? Gratitude acts as a magnet for miracles. It's a transformative power that can turn a regular day into a treasure trove of discoveries and simple moments into memorable events. Imagine if you start by recognizing and acknowledging something beautiful about your life every morning before the day's hustle begins.

The sun streaming through your window, a heartfelt message from a friend, or even the mere act of waking up to a new day - all are reasons to be grateful.

In this chapter, we're about to embark on our second 28-day journey to harness the power of gratitude. Each affirmation will serve as a reminder to cherish what you have, attract positivity, and fundamentally change your perspective on life.

Remember, gratitude isn't just a practice; it's a way of life. Embrace it, and watch as the universe reciprocates with abundance and positivity. As we dive into this month's affirmations, keep an open heart and let gratitude be your guide. Onward, to a more thankful you!

1. **Affirmation:** I am thankful for every moment in my life.

   Recognizing the value of every moment cultivates a deep sense of gratitude, enriching our life experience.

2. **Affirmation:** Gratitude fills my heart and nourishes my soul.

   This affirmation connects gratitude with spiritual well-being, nurturing inner peace.

3. **Affirmation:** I express gratitude for my health, friends, and family.

   By being grateful for essential aspects of life, we create a positive mindset.

4. **Affirmation:** I am open to the abundance of the universe, and I am grateful for all I receive.

   This affirmation aligns us with the universe, inviting prosperity through gratitude.

5. **Affirmation:** My gratitude for today paves the way for tomorrow's blessings.

   Appreciating today's blessings lays a positive foundation for future abundance.

6. **Affirmation:** I am grateful for my mistakes, for they have taught me valuable lessons.

   This affirmation turns mistakes into learning opportunities, fostering growth.

7. **Affirmation:** I appreciate the love and support that surrounds me every day.

   Recognizing the love and support in our lives strengthens connections and spreads positivity.

8. **Affirmation:** I am thankful for my strength, resilience, and courage.

   Gratitude for inner qualities builds self-confidence and empowers us to face challenges.

9. **Affirmation:** I embrace gratitude in all areas of my life.

   This affirmation fosters a holistic approach to gratitude, encompassing all life aspects.

10. **Affirmation:** I am grateful for nature's beauty and the joy it brings me.

    Appreciating nature connects us to the world around us and enhances overall well-being.

11. **Affirmation:** I am grateful for my dreams and the inspiration they provide.

    Valuing our dreams aligns us with our passions and goals.

12. **Affirmation:** I express gratitude effortlessly and genuinely.

    This affirmation helps cultivate an authentic and natural expression of gratitude.

13. **Affirmation:** I am thankful for the opportunities that challenge me.

Gratitude for challenges promotes personal growth and a positive perspective on life.

14. **Affirmation:** My heart overflows with gratitude, joy, and love.

Cultivating these positive emotions leads to a more fulfilling and enriched life.

15. **Affirmation:** I am grateful for the present moment and all its teachings.

Embracing the present moment with gratitude enhances mindfulness and contentment.

16. **Affirmation:** I am thankful for the future and all the possibilities it holds.

Looking forward to the future with gratitude instills hope and optimism.

17. **Affirmation:** My gratitude shines through my actions and words.

This affirmation encourages us to express gratitude actively and positively.

18. **Affirmation:** I appreciate my journey and all the experiences it encompasses.

Gratitude for life's journey, including its ups and downs, fosters wisdom and acceptance.

19. **Affirmation:** My gratitude is a magnet for miracles.

Belief in the power of gratitude can manifest remarkable changes in our lives.

20. **Affirmation:** I am grateful for laughter, joy, and happiness.

Appreciating these positive emotions contributes to a joyful life.

21. **Affirmation:** I value and express gratitude for my unique talents and abilities.

    Recognizing personal strengths and being thankful for them enhances self-worth.

22. **Affirmation:** I am grateful for the kindness and compassion of others.

    Acknowledging the goodness in others promotes a positive and connected community.

23. **Affirmation:** My gratitude extends beyond myself, touching others.

    This affirmation emphasizes the far-reaching effects of gratitude, fostering empathy and connection.

24. **Affirmation:** I am thankful for the comfort and safety of my home.

    Gratitude for fundamental necessities enhances contentment and security.

25. **Affirmation:** I appreciate my growth, knowing each step leads me forward.

    Being grateful for personal growth recognizes progress and encourages perseverance.

26. **Affirmation:** I am grateful for my body and all that it allows me to do.

    This affirmation fosters a positive body image and overall well-being.

27. **Affirmation:** My gratitude connects me to a higher purpose.

    This affirmation aligns gratitude with a deeper, more profound sense of meaning and direction.

28. **Affirmation:** I radiate gratitude, attracting positive energy and abundance.

    Emphasizing the transformative power of gratitude, this affirmation encourages us to spread positivity and attract goodness into our lives.

These affirmations, with their respective motivations, form a powerful guide to help you cultivate gratitude in various aspects of your daily life. Each affirmation encourages mindfulness, appreciation, and a deep connection to oneself and the world, aligning perfectly with the chapter's theme.

CHAPTER 3:
Building Confidence

"Our deepest fear is not that we are inadequate. Our deepest fear is that we are powerful beyond measure." - Marianne Williamson.

Have you ever gazed at a skyscraper, marveling at its grandeur? Each of those towering marvels started with a single brick. Just like them, the most unwavering self-confidence begins with a tiny seed of belief. Your journey into this chapter is akin to laying that foundational brick, paving the path towards an unshakeable self-belief.

Confidence isn't merely about walking with your head held high or speaking without hesitation. It's about the inner voice that says, "I can," even when the world whispers, "You can't." However, for many of us, that voice has been drowned out over the years. Be it by past failures, societal expectations, or even self-imposed limitations, we've sometimes forgotten our inherent worth.

This chapter is your wake-up call.

Consider this: Within each of us lies an immense potential, often untapped and unacknowledged. Remember those moments when you achieved something you initially deemed impossible? That was not a fluke; that was you tapping into a tiny fraction of your potential. Now, imagine harnessing that power daily. That's what building confidence can achieve.

The affirmations in this chapter are meticulously crafted to remind you of your worth and help you see your potential in a new light. They are your daily nudge, your gentle reminder that the power you seek externally has been within you all along.

As you embark on this month of affirmations, recognize that you are not creating a new You, but rediscovering the powerful, confident individual who's been there all along, waiting to emerge. This is your time. Embrace it. Own it. Believe in it. 🚀

Let's begin.

1. **Affirmation**: I believe in myself and my abilities.

   This affirmation fuels self-belief, creating a foundation for achieving anything you set your mind to. It emphasizes that you are capable and empowers you to take on challenges.

2. **Affirmation**: I am confident, strong, and capable.

   Repeating this affirmation reinforces the understanding of your inner strength, leading to more decisive actions and success in your personal and professional life.

3. **Affirmation**: I face fear and uncertainty with courage.

   This affirmation promotes the courage to tackle uncomfortable situations, leading to personal growth and the ability to overcome future obstacles.

4. **Affirmation**: I trust my intuition and make wise decisions.

   This affirmation guides the decision-making process by instilling trust in oneself, allowing you to rely on your instincts to make sound choices.

5. **Affirmation**: I radiate confidence, and others respect me.

   By exuding confidence, you command respect from others. This affirmation reinforces a confident demeanor, affecting how others perceive and respond to you.

6. **Affirmation**: I embrace challenges as opportunities.

   This affirmation shifts the mindset towards challenges, seeing them as opportunities to learn and grow, enhancing your overall confidence in handling life's ups and downs.

7. **Affirmation**: I confidently speak my truth and stand my ground.

   Encouraging you to express yourself authentically, this affirmation emphasizes the importance of being genuine, honest, and confident in your convictions.

8. **Affirmation**: I am worthy of success, and I pursue my goals fearlessly.

   This affirmation propels you to chase your dreams without fear, reinforcing the belief that you are deserving of success and capable of achieving it.

9. **Affirmation**: My confidence grows every day.

   Confidence is a journey, not a destination. This affirmation acknowledges that growth and development are continuous processes, fostering continual improvement.

10. **Affirmation**: I am confident in my decisions and learn from my mistakes.

    Mistakes are inevitable, but this affirmation emphasizes the importance of learning from them and building confidence through wisdom gained from experience.

11. **Affirmation**: I accept myself unconditionally and know my worth.

    Self-acceptance is vital for confidence. This affirmation encourages embracing yourself entirely and recognizing your unique value and worth.

12. **Affirmation**: I take bold steps, knowing I have the strength to succeed.

Encouraging boldness and courage, this affirmation assures you that you have the inner strength to succeed in whatever you undertake.

13. **Affirmation**: I am in charge of my life and my path.

Emphasizing personal empowerment, this affirmation enables you to take control of your destiny, reinforcing confidence in your life's journey.

14. **Affirmation**: I celebrate my victories, no matter how small.

Celebrating even minor achievements can foster greater self-confidence. This affirmation reminds you to acknowledge and honor your successes.

15. **Affirmation**: I exude confidence, charm, and grace.

Embracing these qualities, this affirmation supports a more confident demeanor in social interactions, and building self-assurance in various settings.

16. **Affirmation**: I release all doubts and trust myself completely.

Doubts can cripple confidence. This affirmation supports letting go of doubt and trusting in yourself, allowing you to move forward with assurance.

17. **Affirmation**: I am proud of who I am and how far I've come.

Recognizing and appreciating your progress boosts confidence, and this affirmation reminds you of your accomplishments and personal growth.

18. **Affirmation**: I am resilient and bounce back with vigor.

Emphasizing resilience, this affirmation assures you that you can recover from setbacks, strengthening your confidence in handling life's adversities.

19. **Affirmation**: I am competent, smart, and can handle all situations.

A wide-reaching affirmation, this boosts confidence across various aspects of life, assuring you that you can handle whatever comes your way.

20. **Affirmation**: I empower others, and I am empowered by them.

Confidence doesn't exist in isolation; this affirmation emphasizes mutual empowerment, strengthening relationships and self-assurance simultaneously.

21. **Affirmation**: I am self-reliant and capable of achieving my dreams.

Emphasizing self-reliance, this affirmation strengthens belief in your abilities, reinforcing that you can achieve your dreams without undue dependence on others.

22. **Affirmation**: I trust in my abilities and express myself confidently.

Supporting confident self-expression, this affirmation fosters assurance in communicating ideas and feelings, promoting personal authenticity.

23. **Affirmation**: I am unstoppable, and nothing can hold me back.

Infusing a strong sense of determination, this affirmation reinforces the belief that you can overcome obstacles and pursue your path with unwavering confidence.

24. **Affirmation**: I am unique, and my voice matters.

Encouraging self-acceptance, this affirmation emphasizes the value of individuality and the importance of expressing your unique perspective.

25. **Affirmation**: I approach life with confidence and enthusiasm.

Bringing energy and zeal to daily life, this affirmation encourages a positive and confident approach to all activities and interactions.

26. **Affirmation**: I am prepared for success and embrace it with open arms.

This affirmation prepares you for success by encouraging a confident and open mindset, allowing you to embrace opportunities as they come.

27. **Affirmation**: I value myself and recognize my greatness.

Self-recognition and appreciation fuel confidence, and this affirmation encourages you to see and celebrate your inherent greatness.

28. **Affirmation**: I am a beacon of confidence, and I shine brightly.

Serving as a strong metaphor, this affirmation inspires you to let your confidence shine, positively impacting those around you and enhancing your self-assurance.

These affirmations are carefully crafted to lay the foundation of positive self-discovery by building confidence with each passing affirmation. As you grow in confidence and begin to embrace the possibility of change, you will begin to discover more about yourself than you knew.

CHAPTER 4:
Overcoming Challenges

The Journey of a Thousand Miles

Have you ever stopped in your tracks, overwhelmed by the weight of life's challenges, and wondered, "Why does this always happen to me?" We've all been there, facing towering mountains that seem impossible to climb. From unexpected setbacks at work to personal struggles that test our emotional resilience, life sometimes feels like an obstacle course designed just for us.

However, an age-old saying goes, "The journey of a thousand miles begins with a single step." Think about it. Every significant achievement, every mountaintop reached, and every triumphant moment has its roots in a simple, yet determined step forward.

The beauty of the human spirit lies not in the absence of challenges but in our ability to overcome them. For in those challenges, in those stumbling blocks, we discover the depth of our strength, the reach of our courage, and the resilience of our spirit.

This chapter is your guide to embracing every challenge, be it big or small, with confidence and determination. The affirmations within these pages are not magic spells that will make your problems disappear, but they are tools to shift your mindset. They are the whispers of encouragement that say, "Yes, it's tough. But so are you."

Let's embark on this journey together, reaffirming your belief in your capabilities and embracing the lessons hidden in every challenge. With each affirmation, you'll feel a newfound sense of power, realizing that the only mountains you can't overcome are the ones you never attempt to climb.

Are you ready to transform challenges into stepping stones? Let's begin. 💪🧗

1. **Affirmation**: I embrace challenges as opportunities for growth.

    Embracing challenges as learning opportunities rather than hindrances leads to a more resilient and adaptive mindset. It helps one see beyond the obstacle and focus on the potential growth and wisdom gained.

2. **Affirmation**: I am stronger than any obstacle in my path.

    This affirmation empowers the belief in one's strength and ability to overcome anything. It fuels determination and confidence that no matter how big the obstacle, it can be conquered.

3. **Affirmation**: Every challenge brings me closer to my goals.

    Understanding that each challenge is a stepping stone towards achieving your dreams helps maintain motivation and focus. It aligns the struggle with the end goal, making it a part of the success journey.

4. **Affirmation**: I have the courage to face and conquer my fears.

    Courage is essential to face challenges, especially when they are rooted in fear. This affirmation aids in building the bravery needed to confront and overcome those fears.

5. **Affirmation**: I trust in my abilities to find solutions.

    Trusting in one's abilities fosters confidence in problem-solving. This affirmation strengthens the belief in oneself to find innovative and effective solutions to any challenge.

6. **Affirmation**: Challenges are temporary; my perseverance is permanent.

This affirmation emphasizes that while challenges may come and go, the determination and persistence to overcome them remain constant. It helps maintain a long-term perspective.

90-Day Milestone Celebration: A Journey of Positivity and Growth

Congratulations! You've reached the 90-day mark in your transformative journey with "Wake Up with Positivity."

This isn't just a milestone; it's a testament to your dedication, persistence, and commitment to fostering a positive mindset. Over the last three months, you've taken significant steps toward improving your self-belief, confidence, and overall perspective towards life.

Every morning, you woke up, dived into the day's affirmation, and started the day with purpose and positivity. Those daily seeds of positivity have now grown into a garden of self-assuredness, joy, and resilience.

To celebrate this incredible achievement, here's a suggested action plan to make the most of this 90-day milestone:

1. **Reflect and Rejoice:**

   - Take a moment to reflect on your favorite affirmations from the past 90 days. Which ones resonated with you the most?

   - Celebrate your consistency. Whether you've practiced the affirmations daily or occasionally, acknowledge the effort and commitment you've shown.

2. **Share Your Journey:**

   - Talk to a close friend or family member about your experience. Sharing can amplify the joy and the sense of achievement.

- Consider posting your journey on social media with the hashtag #WakeUpWithPositivity to connect with fellow readers and share inspiration.

3. **Revisit and Renew:**

   - Go back to affirmations that deeply resonated with you or ones you felt were particularly challenging. The repetition can strengthen their impact.

   - Consider setting a new personal goal or challenge related to positivity and self-growth for the next 90 days.

4. **Journal Your Growth:**

   - Document your feelings, accomplishments, and any changes you've noticed in your mindset or life over these three months.

   - Journaling is a great way to track progress and keep yourself motivated for the next leg of your journey.

5. **Reward Yourself:**

   - Treat yourself to something you love. It could be a day off, a special treat, a new book, or even just some quiet time to relax and be proud of yourself.

And now, as you embark on the next phase of your journey, remember this motivational quote:

"The journey of a thousand miles begins with one step." - Lao Tzu

Continue taking those steps every day, nurturing your garden of positivity, and embracing the wonderful changes that unfold. Here's to your unwavering spirit, continued growth, and many more milestones ahead! 👁 🚀 🧭

1. **Affirmation**: I learn from each challenge and become wiser.

   Challenges are seen as teachers in this affirmation. The learning and wisdom gained from overcoming obstacles make one stronger and better prepared for future challenges.

2. **Affirmation**: I am grateful for challenges; they shape my character.

   Gratitude for challenges helps foster a positive attitude towards them. Recognizing that they shape character and resilience helps to embrace them with a growth mindset.

3. **Affirmation**: I am in control of how I respond to challenges.

   Emphasizing control over reactions empowers one to choose a constructive and positive response to challenges. It encourages responsibility and ownership of one's actions.

4. **Affirmation**: I overcome challenges with grace and dignity.

   This affirmation focuses on maintaining self-respect and integrity while navigating difficulties. It helps to keep one grounded and poised even in the face of adversity.

5. **Affirmation**: I attract positive energy that helps me overcome difficulties.

   Attracting positivity is the focus, and by doing so, this affirmation helps maintain an optimistic outlook during challenging times. It encourages a positive environment that fosters success.

6. **Affirmation**: I am patient with myself during challenging times.

   Patience with oneself during challenges is essential for self-compassion and mindfulness. This affirmation helps to maintain balance and prevent burnout.

7. **Affirmation**: I focus on solutions, not problems.

   Shifting focus from problems to solutions fosters a proactive approach. This affirmation encourages the creative thinking needed to overcome challenges effectively.

8. **Affirmation**: I face challenges with a heart full of courage.

   Courage from within is a powerful ally in facing challenges. This affirmation nurtures the emotional strength required to stand tall against any obstacle.

9. **Affirmation**: I believe in the timing of my life, including its challenges.

   Trusting in the timing and natural flow of life helps one embrace challenges as part of the journey. This affirmation reinforces the acceptance and understanding of life's pace.

10. **Affirmation**: I grow through what I go through.

    Emphasizing growth through experiences, this affirmation helps one appreciate the transformative power of challenges. It encourages a perspective shift towards personal development.

11. **Affirmation**: I am resilient, and nothing can keep me down.

    Resilience is a key attribute for overcoming challenges. This affirmation instills a sense of indomitable spirit and perseverance.

12. **Affirmation**: My struggles are my stepping stones to success.

    Viewing struggles as part of the success path helps maintain motivation. This affirmation helps align challenges with the ultimate goal of achievement and success.

13. **Affirmation**: Challenges do not define me; they refine me.

Challenges are transformative rather than defining. This affirmation emphasizes personal growth and refinement as a result of overcoming obstacles.

14. **Affirmation**: I choose to see challenges as invitations to evolve.

    Viewing challenges as opportunities for personal evolution fosters a positive approach. This affirmation aids in embracing challenges as catalysts for growth.

15. **Affirmation**: I remain calm and composed in the face of difficulties.

    Maintaining calmness in adversity aids in clear thinking and decision-making. This affirmation reinforces the importance of emotional balance during challenging times.

16. **Affirmation**: I celebrate my victories, big or small, over challenges.

    Recognizing and celebrating victories encourages positive reinforcement. This affirmation helps one appreciate progress, no matter how small, in overcoming challenges.

17. **Affirmation**: I am unstoppable in my pursuit of overcoming obstacles.

    An affirmation of unyielding determination, this statement helps fuel the relentless pursuit of overcoming any obstacles in one's path.

18. **Affirmation**: I transform challenges into lessons and success.

    This affirmation focuses on the transformation of challenges into positive outcomes. It encourages learning and personal growth from every obstacle faced.

19. **Affirmation**: I have everything I need within me to succeed.

    Emphasizing inner strength and resources, this affirmation instills confidence that all necessary tools for success are already within oneself.

20. **Affirmation**: I am guided by a higher power in overcoming challenges.

    For those with spiritual beliefs, this affirmation may strengthen the connection to a higher power or universal guidance in facing life's difficulties.

21. **Affirmation**: I radiate positivity that helps me conquer any challenge.

    By focusing on radiating positivity, this affirmation helps maintain a positive attitude and energy that are essential for conquering any challenge.

22. **Affirmation**: My journey through challenges is a testament to my strength.

    This final affirmation in the chapter serves as a declaration of strength and resilience, acknowledging the power of one's journey through challenges as a reflection of one's inner fortitude.

These affirmations, tailored to overcoming challenges, empower you to approach obstacles with confidence, wisdom, and a positive mindset. They provide daily encouragement and insight to help transform challenges into opportunities for growth and success.

CHAPTER 5:
Mindful Living

The rhythmic chime of a meditation bell resonates through a silent room, punctuating the stillness, and reminding us of the present moment. The here and now. Have you ever paused to consider the miraculous nature of this moment? We are ceaselessly propelled by our memories of the past and our anxieties about the future, often overlooking the true essence of the present moment.

Imagine you're walking down a serene beach. The sun sets in a kaleidoscope of purples and oranges, the waves gently kiss your feet, and the breeze carries the taste of salt. Now imagine being wholly engrossed in this moment, feeling every sensation, relishing every breath. This is mindfulness.

As we journey through the hustle and bustle of urban life, we often forget to 'live.' We become robotic, completing tasks and achieving targets. We're frequently either ruminating on the past or anticipating the future, failing to truly engage with our current experiences. But here's the powerful revelation: Life unfolds in the present. But so often, we let the present slip away, letting time rush past unobserved and squandering the precious seconds of our lives as we worry about the future and ruminate about what's past.

"Life is a dance. Mindfulness is witnessing that dance." - Amit Ray.

By embracing mindfulness, we can transform our daily routines, interactions, and challenges. It's not about escaping reality but rather fully immersing ourselves in it. This chapter, "Mindful Living," is dedicated to helping you anchor yourself in the now. Through the affirmations shared in this section, you'll be equipped to find beauty in the ordinary, joy in the mundane, and above all, peace within the chaos.

As you begin this month-long journey of mindful affirmations, remember: Every moment is a new beginning, a new opportunity. It's a chance to reset, refocus, and truly live. Each affirmation will guide you closer to living a life fully awake, aware, and alive. So, take a deep breath, and let's embark on this transformative journey together, immersing ourselves in the endless beauty of the present moment.

Embrace the power of now. Because right now is the perfect moment to start living mindfully. 🪶💗

1. **Affirmation:** I live in the present moment and embrace the joy it brings.

   This affirmation helps us anchor ourselves in the present, breaking free from the regrets of the past and worries of the future, leading to true inner peace.

2. **Affirmation:** I am connected to the world around me.

   Acknowledging our connection to the world fosters a sense of belonging and compassion, enhancing our mindfulness.

3. **Affirmation:** My breath is my anchor to the present moment.

   The breath serves as a continuous reminder of the present moment, guiding us to a calm and focused state of mind.

4. **Affirmation:** I appreciate the beauty in the ordinary.

   Recognizing the beauty in everyday things enriches our lives and helps us cultivate gratitude.

5. **Affirmation:** I observe my thoughts and emotions without judgment.

By learning to observe without judgment, we gain insights into our behavior and reactions, paving the way for self-growth.

6. **Affirmation:** I cultivate stillness within me.

   Creating a sense of inner calm enhances our mental clarity and well-being, allowing us to respond more mindfully.

7. **Affirmation:** I find joy in silence.

   Embracing silence helps in nurturing mindfulness, providing space for reflection and relaxation.

8. **Affirmation:** I embrace imperfections as part of life's beautiful tapestry.

   This affirmation encourages us to accept life's imperfections, recognizing them as an integral part of our growth and journey.

9. **Affirmation:** I am patient with myself and others.

   Patience fosters kindness and understanding, creating harmonious relationships with ourselves and others.

10. **Affirmation:** I listen deeply and communicate with empathy.

    Mindful listening fosters compassionate and meaningful connections, enhancing our interpersonal relationships.

11. **Affirmation:** I nourish my body with mindful eating.

    Mindful eating enhances our relationship with food and our body, leading to better health and well-being.

12. **Affirmation:** I am aware of my body and honor its needs.

    Connecting with our physical sensations helps us respond to our body's needs, fostering overall health.

13. **Affirmation:** I am at peace with my past.

    Letting go of past grievances liberates us from unnecessary burdens, allowing us to live more fully in the present.

14. **Affirmation:** I accept what I cannot change.

   Acceptance empowers us to focus on what we can control, fostering a sense of peace and clarity.

15. **Affirmation:** I focus on one task at a time.

   Singular focus enhances our productivity and enjoyment of the task at hand, promoting mindfulness in action.

16. **Affirmation:** I make time for quiet reflection.

   Regular moments of reflection encourage self-awareness and growth, deepening our connection to our inner self.

17. **Affirmation:** I value my inner wisdom and intuition.

   Trusting our intuition enhances our decision-making and aligns us with our authentic selves.

18. **Affirmation:** I find balance in my daily life.

   Cultivating balance fosters a harmonious lifestyle, enriching our well-being and satisfaction.

19. **Affirmation:** I am kind to myself in my thoughts and actions.

   Self-kindness creates a nurturing inner environment, boosting self-esteem and well-being.

20. **Affirmation:** I embrace simplicity in my life.

   Simplicity brings clarity and focus, reducing unnecessary stress and enhancing our overall quality of life.

21. **Affirmation:** I am in harmony with the universe.

   Feeling aligned with the universe fosters a sense of purpose and interconnectedness, enhancing our spiritual well-being.

22. **Affirmation:** I approach challenges with mindfulness and calm.

Mindful reactions to challenges lead to wiser choices and outcomes, reducing stress and frustration.

23. **Affirmation:** I cultivate mindfulness through regular practice.

Regular mindfulness practice enhances our mental clarity, focus, and emotional balance, contributing to a richer life experience.

24. **Affirmation:** I respect and honor my emotions.

Accepting and respecting our emotions without judgment fosters emotional intelligence and well-being.

25. **Affirmation:** I cherish the present, for it's a gift.

Recognizing the present as a unique and unrepeatable moment fosters gratitude and joy.

26. **Affirmation:** I radiate calmness and serenity.

Cultivating inner serenity enhances our relationships, work, and overall life experience as we become a calming presence for others.

27. **Affirmation:** I lead with compassion and understanding.

Compassionate leadership fosters empathy and collaboration, enhancing our connections with others.

28. **Affirmation:** I am the creator of my peaceful and joyful reality.

Recognizing ourselves as creators empowers us to shape our lives actively, leading to fulfillment and happiness.

Mindful living enriches our existence by helping us connect more deeply with ourselves, others, and the world around us. These affirmations serve as daily reminders to cultivate awareness, compassion, and inner peace, providing a pathway to a more mindful and fulfilling life. 🧘♂️□

CHAPTER 6:
Nurturing Relationships

The subtle hum of a café in the heart of the city; two individuals lost deep in conversation, their faces lit up with smiles and understanding. The joy of a child's first steps is captured through the beaming eyes of family. The reassuring hand of a friend, reaching out during times of turmoil. The strength of relationships, both profound and simple, shapes our lives in ways we often underestimate.

Have you ever stopped to consider the incredible impact relationships have on our lives? We are, by nature, social beings. From the cavemen days, surviving and thriving in groups, to our modern interconnected world, our relationships define us. They provide us with joy, support, challenges, and learning. In essence, they serve as mirrors reflecting our virtues, our flaws, and our growth.

"The quality of your life is the quality of your relationships." This profound statement by Tony Robbins encapsulates the essence of our existence. And yet, in the hustle and grind of modern life, we often neglect the very relationships that fuel our souls. It's not just about building relationships but nurturing them, making them thrive amidst the chaos.

Now, imagine starting your day with an affirmation that strengthens the bond you share with your loved ones. An affirmation that reminds you of the importance of meaningful connections, of the joy in shared laughter, of the comfort in a shoulder to lean on. How would that change your perspective on life? How would that elevate your daily experiences?

In this chapter, we embark on a transformative journey of affirmations centered around relationships. From deepening our existing bonds to forming new, meaningful connections, every affirmation will serve as a beacon of love, understanding, and mutual respect.

As we venture into this realm of relationships, keep in mind a beautiful African proverb: "If you want to go fast, go alone. If you want to go far, go together." Let's nurture our 'together' and enrich the tapestry of our lives.

Dive in, dear reader, and discover the magic that lies in the heart of every relationship. Let these affirmations guide you to a world of deeper connections and heartfelt moments. 🗿 💝 🌍

1. **Affirmation**: I am open to understanding and accepting others for who they are.
   Embracing this affirmation encourages empathy and acceptance in relationships, which can lead to deeper connections with others.

2. **Affirmation**: I express my love and appreciation freely and honestly.

   By expressing love and appreciation openly, we build trust and strengthen the emotional bonds in relationships.

3. **Affirmation**: I am a good listener and value others' opinions.

   Listening is key to understanding others and respecting their perspectives, fostering a more supportive and caring relationship.

4. **Affirmation**: I am committed to growing and nurturing my relationships every day.

Commitment to growth in relationships helps maintain a healthy connection and shows that we value our relationships.

5. **Affirmation**: I attract loving and supportive relationships into my life.

   This affirmation aligns our energy to attract relationships that are fulfilling and nourishing.

6. **Affirmation**: I am forgiving and understanding in my relationships.

   Forgiveness and understanding are crucial in healing and maintaining long-term relationships.

7. **Affirmation**: My relationships are a reflection of mutual respect and trust.

   Affirming mutual respect and trust helps solidify the foundation of a healthy relationship.

8. **Affirmation**: I celebrate the successes and joys of those I love.

   Supporting and celebrating others' successes fosters a loving and encouraging relationship environment.

9. **Affirmation**: I am grateful for the love and support I receive from others.

   Gratitude for love and support reinforces positive feelings and connections with others.

10. **Affirmation**: I communicate my feelings honestly and kindly.

    Open and kind communication ensures clarity and compassion in relationships.

11. **Affirmation**: I invest time and energy in the relationships that matter to me.

Investing in relationships shows that we prioritize and value them, leading to deeper connections.

12. **Affirmation**: I am worthy of love and connection.

Recognizing our worthiness of love helps us engage in relationships with confidence and self-respect.

13. **Affirmation**: I support others without judgment.

Offering non-judgmental support fosters trust and acceptance in relationships.

14. **Affirmation**: I am loving and accepting of myself, just as I am.

Self-love is foundational to all relationships, setting a standard for how we wish to be treated by others.

15. **Affirmation**: I embrace the uniqueness of my relationships.

Embracing uniqueness celebrates diversity and promotes acceptance in various types of relationships.

16. **Affirmation**: I am at peace with my past relationships and open to new ones.

Letting go of past relationship baggage allows for fresh starts and new connections.

17. **Affirmation**: I grow through relationships, both pleasant and challenging.

Recognizing growth through all kinds of relationships fosters resilience and wisdom.

18. **Affirmation**: My relationships are a source of comfort and joy.

Focusing on the positive aspects of relationships nurtures a joyful connection.

19. **Affirmation**: I set healthy boundaries in my relationships.

    Setting boundaries ensures respect and understanding, maintaining a balanced and healthy relationship.

20. **Affirmation**: I see the best in others and encourage their potential.

    Encouraging potential and seeing the best in others fosters a positive and uplifting relationship dynamic.

21. **Affirmation**: I am patient with myself and others in my relationships.

    Patience is key to understanding and compassion, allowing relationships to flourish even during challenging times.

22. **Affirmation**: My heart is open to giving and receiving love.

    An open heart promotes a free flow of love and connection, enhancing our relationships.

23. **Affirmation**: I am committed to resolving conflicts with understanding and compassion.

    Commitment to resolving conflicts positively ensures the long-term health and success of relationships.

24. **Affirmation**: I cherish and honor the connections I have with family and friends.

    Cherishing connections nurtures a sense of belonging and love within our closest relationships.

25. **Affirmation**: My love for others is unconditional and pure.

    Unconditional love is the cornerstone of deeply connected and fulfilling relationships.

26. **Affirmation**: I nurture my relationships with time, effort, and genuine affection.

Regular nurturing of relationships strengthens bonds and demonstrates love and commitment.

27. **Affirmation**: I trust in the goodness and sincerity of those around me.

Trust is the foundation of any strong relationship, and it begins with believing in the goodness of others.

28. **Affirmation**: My relationships enrich my life and bring me joy.

Acknowledging the enrichment and joy from relationships fosters a positive and grateful attitude towards our connections.

These affirmations serve as gentle reminders and guideposts for building and maintaining healthy, loving, and supportive relationships in all areas of life. Whether applied to friendships, family, or intimate connections, they can lead to a more balanced, joyful, and fulfilling relationship experience.

Halfway Milestone:
Celebrating Your Positive Journey

As you turn the pages to this midpoint in your journey with "Wake Up with Positivity," let's take a moment to celebrate how far you've come!

By now, you've journeyed through self-love, gratitude, confidence, and much more. You've been armed with affirmations that act as a shield against negativity and a catalyst for positive transformation.

✷ **Highlight of Your Journey Thus Far**:

- **Embraced Self-love**: You've started acknowledging and loving yourself more deeply.

- **Cultivated Gratitude**: You've learned the art of being thankful for life's many blessings.

- **Boosted Confidence**: You've begun to see yourself in a new light, believing in your capabilities.

- **Grew Resilient**: Challenges no longer deter you; rather, they fuel your growth.

- **Embarked on Mindfulness**: Living in the present moment is becoming your second nature.

- **Nurtured Relationships**: Strengthening bonds and creating positive ripple effects in the lives of those around you.

Remember, every morning you chose to recite an affirmation, you took a step closer to the best version of yourself. The commitment and effort you've shown are nothing short of commendable.

As a token of this celebration, here's an inspirational quote to keep you motivated for the journey ahead:

"The future belongs to those who believe in the beauty of their dreams." - **Eleanor Roosevelt**

Your journey is only half complete, yet look at the progress you've made! Here's to forging ahead with the same vigor, enthusiasm, and positivity. The road ahead is promising, and with each day, you're getting closer to your goal of lasting positivity and personal transformation. Let's continue this beautiful journey together!

CHAPTER 7:
Healthy Habits for Body and Mind

The morning sun stretches across the horizon, casting its warm golden hues. Just as the sun rejuvenates the world with its light, our body and mind seek daily nourishment. Often, we're engrossed in the fast pace of life, chasing deadlines, and ticking off to-do lists. But, have you ever paused and pondered about the vessel that's enabling you to pursue these dreams? That powerful engine that drives your aspirations? It's your body and mind.

The connection between our physical self and our mental state is profound, interwoven in ways we sometimes neglect. Think about the times you've felt mentally drained after a physically exhausting day or the restless nights after a day of stress. The two are inextricably linked, each impacting the other in a perpetual dance of well-being.

Now, imagine a world where you wake up, not to the blaring alarms and instant stress, but to a symphony of positive affirmations. A world where every muscle stretch, every deep breath, every nutritious bite is accompanied by a positive thought. The ripple effect it would create in your overall well-being is boundless.

"Our bodies are our gardens to which our wills are gardeners." This quote by William Shakespeare underscores the essence of this chapter. We have the tools, the seeds, the soil, and the water. But how do we cultivate this garden, ensuring it's lush, vibrant, and evergreen?

In this chapter, we're diving deep into a month-long journey of intertwining physical well-being with mental fortitude. These affirmations are crafted not just for the soul but for the very vessel that houses it. As we venture through these affirmations, remember: every time you fuel your body with good health, you're also fueling your mind with positivity.

Let's embark on this enlightening journey, strengthening our body and mind with the power of positive affirmations. After all, a sound mind in a sound body isn't just an old adage; it's a lifestyle. 🏃 🧠 💪

Ready to nurture both your body and mind? Let the affirmations begin!

1. **Affirmation**: I prioritize my physical health through nourishing food and regular exercise.
    Feeding your body with nourishing food and engaging in physical activity fuels your overall well-being and creates a strong foundation for a positive life.

2. **Affirmation**: I am in tune with my body and listen to what it needs.

    Listening to your body's needs fosters self-awareness and helps you make choices that align with your health and well-being.

3. **Affirmation**: I nurture my mental well-being with self-care and relaxation.

    Caring for your mental well-being through relaxation and self-care practices contributes to emotional balance and overall happiness.

4. **Affirmation**: I embrace quality sleep as essential for my mind and body to rejuvenate.

    Quality sleep is paramount for rejuvenation, playing a vital role in maintaining both mental clarity and physical vitality.

5. **Affirmation**: My body is a temple, and I treat it with respect and love.

Honoring and respecting your body fosters a positive relationship with yourself and encourages mindful decisions regarding health.

6. **Affirmation**: I am committed to a consistent fitness routine that empowers me.

   Engaging in regular exercise strengthens your body and mind, enhancing your overall sense of empowerment and accomplishment.

7. **Affirmation**: I drink plenty of water to hydrate my body and mind.

   Proper hydration nourishes your body at a cellular level, supporting physical function and mental clarity.

8. **Affirmation**: I make mindful eating choices that nourish my body.

   Mindful eating fosters a deeper connection with your body's needs and encourages nutritional choices that promote overall health.

9. **Affirmation**: I breathe deeply to center myself and calm my mind.

   Deep breathing is a powerful tool for calming the mind and body, aiding in relaxation and stress reduction.

10. **Affirmation**: I find joy in movement and celebrate my body's capabilities.

    Embracing the joy of movement and celebrating your body's abilities fosters a positive attitude towards fitness and health.

11. **Affirmation**: I allow myself to rest without guilt, knowing it's vital for my well-being.

Rest is a crucial component of a balanced lifestyle, allowing both mind and body to recover and rejuvenate without guilt or pressure.

12. **Affirmation**: My mental health is as important as my physical health, and I care for both.

Recognizing the equal importance of mental and physical health promotes a holistic approach to well-being, nurturing all aspects of yourself.

13. **Affirmation**: I am open to new healthy habits that align with my well-being.

Being open to new healthy habits encourages growth and adaptability, leading to a more fulfilling and balanced lifestyle.

14. **Affirmation**: I am gentle with myself and recognize that my body's needs may change.

Being gentle and understanding of your body's changing needs promotes self-compassion and mindfulness in your health journey.

15. **Affirmation**: I find balance in my life by honoring my mental and physical needs.

Seeking balance by acknowledging both mental and physical needs fosters harmony within yourself, contributing to a holistic sense of well-being.

16. **Affirmation**: I consciously avoid habits that may harm my body or mind.

Consciously avoiding harmful habits protects your overall health and well-being, guiding you towards choices that nourish and sustain you.

17. **Affirmation**: I fill my mind with positive thoughts to support my mental well-being.

    Nurturing your mind with positive thoughts cultivates mental well-being, creating a supportive mental environment for overall happiness.

18. **Affirmation**: I recognize that my health is an investment, not an expense.

    Viewing health as an investment rather than an expense shifts your perspective, recognizing the long-term value of caring for yourself.

19. **Affirmation**: I honor my body with a movement that feels joyful and fulfilling.

    Choosing a joyful and fulfilling movement encourages a positive relationship with exercise and motivates continued engagement.

20. **Affirmation**: I embrace the connection between mind, body, and spirit.

    Embracing the interconnectedness of mind, body, and spirit fosters a comprehensive approach to health, recognizing the wholeness of your being.

21. **Affirmation**: I fuel my body with nutrients that energize and revitalize me.

    Fueling your body with nourishing nutrients provides energy and revitalization, supporting optimal function and vitality.

22. **Affirmation**: I celebrate my progress in my health journey and remain patient with myself.

    Celebrating progress and practicing patience on your health journey fosters self-compassion and recognition of your efforts.

23. **Affirmation**: I surround myself with positive influences that support my well-being.

Surrounding yourself with positive influences creates an environment that supports and encourages your commitment to well-being.

24. **Affirmation**: I focus on what feels good for my body and mind rather than societal pressures.

Focusing on what feels good for you, rather than conforming to societal pressures, empowers authentic choices that align with your unique needs and desires.

25. **Affirmation**: I release stress through activities that I enjoy and find calming.

Engaging in activities that you enjoy and find calming is an effective way to release stress and enhance overall wellness.

26. **Affirmation**: I am proactive in seeking professional health advice when needed.

Being proactive in seeking professional health advice when needed demonstrates a responsible and empowered approach to your well-being.

27. **Affirmation**: I recognize the power of a positive mindset in my health journey.

Recognizing the power of positivity in your health journey underscores the profound influence of mindset in shaping overall well-being.

28. **Affirmation**: I create a nurturing environment for myself, filled with self-love and self-care.

29. Creating a nurturing environment for self-love and self-care supports your overall well-being and fosters a loving and compassionate relationship with yourself.

These affirmations provide a daily touchstone for you to cultivate a balanced lifestyle that honors both your mental and physical well-being. Through conscious choices and mindful practices, you will be empowered to create a nurturing and healthy life for yourself.

CHAPTER 8:
Embracing Change

A wise philosopher once remarked, "The only constant in life is change." For many of us, these words elicit a sigh of recognition. We see change swirling all around us, from the rapid pace of technological advancements to the inevitable shifts in our personal lives. Sometimes, we're swept up in its currents, feeling a mixture of excitement, uncertainty, and sometimes, resistance.

But why do we, as adaptable human beings, often resist change? Especially when change is nature's way of ensuring growth. A tree sheds its leaves in the fall to make way for new ones in the spring. A butterfly emerges only after undergoing transformation within its cocoon. Change, in many ways, is a signal that we're alive, evolving, and growing.

Embracing change is about recognizing its inherent value and harnessing its power. The journey through this chapter will equip you with affirmations that encourage flexibility, foster courage, and inspire an open mindset. Through these affirmations, you'll learn to weather life's changes and even welcome them as opportunities for growth, understanding, and rejuvenation.

Starting each day of this month with a focused affirmation about embracing change will act like the gentle nudge we often need. The nudge reminds us that stepping out of our comfort zone is where the magic truly happens. Remember, our lives do not get better by chance but by change. So, let's start this transformative journey together.

Embrace the change, seize the opportunities, and let's dive into a month of growth and newfound strength. 🪁 🦋

"The secret of change is to focus all of your energy, not on fighting the old, but on building the new." - Socrates.

Are you ready to build the new? Let the journey of affirmations begin!

1. **Affirmation:** I welcome change as a path to growth and transformation.

   This affirmation recognizes that change is a natural and necessary part of life that leads to growth and new possibilities.

2. **Affirmation:** Change opens doors I never knew existed.

   By adopting an optimistic view of change, this affirmation helps people to see new opportunities that they might not have recognized before.

3. **Affirmation:** I adapt to change with grace and confidence.

   This statement empowers individuals to approach change with a positive mindset and assurance in their ability to handle it.

4. **Affirmation:** Every change in my life serves my highest good.

   This affirmation brings awareness that every shift in life, whether perceived as good or bad, can contribute to one's ultimate well-being.

5. **Affirmation:** I let go of fear and embrace the adventure of change.

6. This affirmation helps to replace anxiety and fear with a sense of excitement and adventure when facing change.

7. **Affirmation:** I am flexible and flow with life's twists and turns.

8. Flexibility is key to embracing change, and this affirmation promotes a resilient and adaptable approach to life's ups and downs.

9. **Affirmation:** I trust that everything changes for a reason.

   Understanding that there is often a purpose behind change helps to foster acceptance and trust in the process.

10. **Affirmation:** I am the author of my life, and I choose to write a courageous chapter.

    This affirmation empowers individuals to take charge of their lives and approach changes with bravery and determination.

11. **Affirmation:** Change nourishes my soul and revitalizes my spirit.

    Recognizing change as a revitalizing force can enhance one's spiritual growth and energy.

12. **Affirmation:** I transform fear into curiosity and embrace the unknown.

    Replacing fear with curiosity enables one to approach the unknown with wonder and excitement rather than apprehension.

13. **Affirmation:** Change is a journey, and I am an eager traveler.

    Seeing change as a journey encourages a sense of adventure and exploration, enriching the experience.

14. **Affirmation:** I grow stronger and wiser with every change in my life.

    This affirmation acknowledges that change brings lessons and strengths that contribute to personal wisdom and resilience.

15. **Affirmation:** I let go of old patterns to welcome new opportunities.

    Letting go of old habits and patterns can create space for new growth and opportunities.

16. **Affirmation:** I thrive in new situations and find joy in unexpected paths.

   Emphasizing thriving in new situations helps foster a sense of joy and excitement in unexpected changes.

17. **Affirmation:** Change brings fresh beginnings and exciting challenges.

   By focusing on the positive aspects of change, this affirmation encourages embracing new starts and thrilling endeavors.

18. **Affirmation:** I am courageous in the face of change, knowing that it leads to fulfillment.

   Courage in the face of change underscores the understanding that it can lead to personal fulfillment and satisfaction.

19. **Affirmation:** I trust my intuition to guide me through changes.

   Trusting one's intuition creates a sense of inner guidance and assurance when navigating change.

20. **Affirmation:** Change is a creative process that shapes my unique path.

   Recognizing change as a creative process emphasizes its role in crafting an individual and extraordinary life journey.

21. **Affirmation:** I honor the past and embrace the future with open arms.

   Honoring what has been while eagerly anticipating what lies ahead helps to create a balanced perspective on change.

22. **Affirmation:** I choose to see change as a positive transformation.

   Choosing a positive viewpoint of change shifts the focus from loss or fear to growth and transformation.

23. **Affirmation:** My life is in constant evolution, and I evolve with it.

    Embracing the constant evolution of life fosters a harmonious relationship with change.

24. **Affirmation:** Change empowers me to discover new parts of myself.

    Change can be a tool for self-discovery, revealing new aspects and depths of oneself.

25. **Affirmation:** I am prepared for life's surprises and embrace them with joy.

    Being prepared for life's surprises and changes fosters a joyful and positive approach.

26. **Affirmation:** I create positive change in my life with purpose and clarity.

    This affirmation empowers individuals to intentionally create positive changes, guided by a clear understanding of their goals.

27. **Affirmation:** My response to change defines me, not the change itself.

    Focusing on one's response to change rather than the change itself highlights personal agency and character.

28. **Affirmation:** I replace uncertainty with faith and trust in my journey.

    Replacing uncertainty with faith enables a more peaceful and trusting relationship with life's changes.

29. **Affirmation:** I am at peace with life's impermanence and embrace its dynamic nature.

Finding peace with life's impermanence helps one to fully embrace and appreciate its ever-changing nature.

30. **Affirmation:** I am the master of change, and I create a life I love.

Asserting mastery over change emphasizes control and empowerment in shaping a life filled with love and contentment.

These affirmations serve as a powerful daily guide to transform one's relationship with change, foster resilience, and create a life filled with growth, joy, and fulfillment. 🌱 🐛

CHAPTER 9:
Abundance and Prosperity

The sun rises every morning without fail, scattering its golden rays upon the world, showering us with warmth and light. This everyday miracle, taken for granted by many, is a testament to the universe's endless generosity and abundance. Now, imagine if the universe were a reflection of our innermost beliefs and thoughts. What if the abundance we seek externally begins with a shift in our internal perspective?

Welcome to Chapter 9, a realm where we explore the idea of **Abundance and Prosperity**.

💡 Did you know that many millionaires and successful individuals attribute their wealth not just to hard work but also to an abundance mindset? By believing that the world is full of opportunities, enough to go around for everyone, they align themselves with prosperity and success.

Many of us have grown up with limiting beliefs about money and success. Phrases like "Money doesn't grow on trees" or "Rich people are greedy" may have embedded negative connotations about wealth in our minds. These beliefs, often inherited from previous generations, act as invisible barriers preventing us from experiencing true abundance.

In this chapter, we'll challenge and reframe those beliefs. Each affirmation is a step towards cultivating a mindset that sees the world as a place of limitless potential, where success, wealth, and prosperity are not only possible but also inevitable for those who believe.

Just as the sun continues to rise, generously offering its light and warmth, an infinite reservoir of abundance awaits you. All you have to do is believe, affirm, and align yourself with it.

Take a deep breath. As you exhale, let go of any limiting beliefs and fears. As you embark on this month-long journey of affirmations centered around abundance and prosperity, remind yourself: You deserve every bit of success and prosperity that comes your way.

Let's begin this transformative journey. With each affirmation, envision the barriers melting away, allowing for endless possibilities and opportunities.

After all, in the words of motivational speaker Wayne Dyer: "Abundance is not something we acquire. It's something we tune into." Ready to tune in? Let's dive deep. ✳ ⧉

1. **Affirmation:** I attract abundance and success with my positive energy and actions.

   This affirmation sets the stage for manifesting abundance by aligning thoughts and actions with success. Positive energy acts as a magnet, drawing opportunities toward you.

2. **Affirmation:** I am worthy of all the riches I desire.

   Understanding your worthiness helps to dissolve any guilt or fear associated with desiring abundance, allowing you to fully embrace prosperity.

3. **Affirmation:** I use my wealth to help others and make a positive impact.

   This affirmation reinforces the positive cycle of abundance by encouraging generosity and the intention to use wealth for good.

4. **Affirmation:** I am open to receiving unexpected blessings.

   Being open to surprises fosters a mindset of excitement and anticipation for abundance, inviting unexpected opportunities into your life.

5. **Affirmation:** My success is limitless, and my potential is infinite.

   Recognizing your limitless potential empowers you to aim higher and strive for even greater success without restrictions.

6. **Affirmation:** Every day, I grow more financially secure.

   Focusing on gradual growth builds confidence in your financial stability and encourages patient and consistent progress toward prosperity.

7. **Affirmation:** I am grateful for my current abundance, and I welcome more into my life.

   Gratitude for what you already have sets a foundation for attracting even more, creating a positive feedback loop of abundance.

8. **Affirmation:** Abundance is my natural state of being.

   By believing that abundance is your inherent nature, you remove any subconscious blocks that may have been hindering your prosperity.

9. **Affirmation:** I see opportunities for wealth and success everywhere.

   This affirmation helps sharpen your focus, allowing you to recognize and seize opportunities that align with your goals for success.

10. **Affirmation:** I am aligned with the energy of prosperity and wealth.

Aligning with prosperous energy aligns your thoughts and actions with abundance, creating a synergy that propels you toward your financial goals.

11. **Affirmation:** My positive thoughts and actions lead to my financial success.

Emphasizing the connection between positivity and success reinforces the importance of maintaining a positive attitude in achieving financial goals.

12. **Affirmation:** I release all resistance to money, and I now allow it to flow joyously into my life.

This affirmation aids in releasing subconscious blocks that might be preventing money from flowing into your life, promoting a joyful relationship with wealth.

13. **Affirmation:** My income exceeds my expenses, and I am always financially secure.

By affirming financial security and a positive cash flow, you encourage a mindset of financial responsibility and abundance.

14. **Affirmation:** I invest in myself and in opportunities that bring positive returns.

This statement emphasizes the importance of self-investment and wise decision-making to ensure positive returns and continuous growth.

15. **Affirmation:** I am constantly adding value to others and myself.

Recognizing the value you bring reinforces your worth and encourages you to continue contributing positively to yourself and others.

16. **Affirmation:** Wealth and success are normal for me.

Normalizing wealth and success helps to make them attainable and realistic goals, removing any sense of them being out of reach.

17. **Affirmation:** I handle success and wealth with wisdom and integrity.

This affirmation underlines the importance of ethical behavior in handling success and wealth, ensuring a positive relationship with abundance.

18. **Affirmation:** My prosperity contributes to the prosperity of others.

This statement emphasizes the interconnectedness of success, showing that your prosperity positively affects others, creating a community of abundance.

19. **Affirmation:** I am a money magnet, and prosperity easily flows into my life.

Believing you are a magnet for money encourages a confident attitude towards wealth, attracting more of it into your life.

20. **Affirmation:** My wealth allows me to live freely and joyfully.

This affirmation emphasizes the freedom and joy that wealth can bring, promoting a positive outlook on prosperity.

21. **Affirmation:** I trust that the universe supports my highest good.

Trusting in universal support reinforces faith in your path, aligning you with the highest potential for success and abundance.

22. **Affirmation:** My financial success serves as an inspiration to others.

Recognizing the inspirational power of your success motivates you to achieve even more, knowing that your success can positively influence others.

23. **Affirmation:** I am in control of my financial future.

Emphasizing control over your financial destiny empowers you to take charge of your life, knowing that your decisions lead to prosperity.

24. **Affirmation:** My actions create constant prosperity.

By believing that your actions directly contribute to constant prosperity, you encourage proactive behavior towards achieving financial success.

25. **Affirmation:** I celebrate my abundance and share it freely with others.

Celebrating and sharing abundance fosters a joyous and generous attitude towards wealth, contributing to a positive cycle of prosperity.

26. **Affirmation:** I am thankful for the abundance in my life, and I am ready for more.

Expressing readiness for more abundance while being thankful for current blessings maintains a positive, receptive attitude towards prosperity.

27. **Affirmation:** Abundance flows to me from known and unknown sources.

This affirmation opens you up to receiving from all possible avenues, recognizing that abundance can come from unexpected places.

28. **Affirmation:** I am aligned with the energy of abundance, and I affirm my right to a prosperous life.

This closing affirmation cements the entire chapter's theme, affirming your right to a prosperous life and your alignment with the energy of abundance.

These affirmations are designed to shift your mindset towards abundance and prosperity. By internalizing and practicing these statements daily, you will be better equipped to attract success, wealth, and a fulfilling life. 🚀 💰

CHAPTER 10:
Unleashing Creativity

Did you know that our brain is designed to think creatively? In fact, when confronted with a challenge, certain regions of our brain light up with activity, pushing us to find innovative solutions. But in the daily grind, we often find our creativity stifled, buried under routine tasks and self-doubt. What if you could reawaken that dormant creative genius within you, one affirmation at a time?

Creativity isn't just reserved for artists, musicians, or writers. It's an innate ability that lies within all of us, whether it's finding a new way to solve a problem at work, inventing a game for your child, or simply imagining new possibilities for your life. Embracing creativity can lead to a life filled with excitement, innovation, and fulfillment. And the best part? Every single one of us has a reservoir of creativity waiting to be tapped into.

Imagine waking up each day, eager to bring something new into the world. Imagine the thrill of looking at challenges as exciting puzzles waiting to be solved. This chapter is designed to help you reignite that creative spark. Whether you've always considered yourself a creative person or have never dared to think so, these affirmations will challenge and change those beliefs.

You're about to embark on a journey that will remind you of your innate creative abilities. As you recite and internalize each affirmation, you'll slowly peel away layers of doubt and fear, revealing the innovator within. Remember, creativity is not just about producing art—it's about approaching life with curiosity, enthusiasm, and a willingness to experiment.

Are you ready to unlock the doors of your imagination? Let's dive deep into the realm of endless possibilities and discover the wonders that await.

Every sunrise brings a fresh canvas. With each day, you have the opportunity to paint a new story, a new idea, and a new experience. As you journey through these affirmations, let them be the brushstrokes that add vibrant colors to your life's masterpiece. Embrace the adventure, cherish the process, and most importantly, believe in the power of your own creativity.

Let's begin our exploration and set free the boundless creativity that resides in you. 😊 💡 🚀

1. **Affirmation**: My creativity flows effortlessly, and my ideas are unique and valuable.

   This affirmation recognizes that creativity is a natural aspect of oneself and encourages a belief in the individuality and worth of one's ideas.

2. **Affirmation**: I am open to new ideas and embrace unconventional solutions.

   Being open-minded allows for more innovative thinking and encourages exploring outside the typical boundaries of problem-solving.

3. **Affirmation**: I see inspiration in the world around me and use it to fuel my creativity.

   This affirmation encourages finding inspiration in everyday surroundings, reinforcing the idea that creative sparks can come from anywhere.

4. **Affirmation**: My imagination is boundless, and I explore ideas without limitations.

   By believing in the unlimited power of imagination, one allows creativity to thrive without constraints.

5. **Affirmation**: I am unafraid to express my creative thoughts and share them with others.

   Encouraging the courage to share creative ideas helps in gaining feedback and collaboration, leading to further growth and refinement.

6. **Affirmation**: Creativity is a joyful process, and I revel in my artistic expression.

   Emphasizing the joy in creativity fosters a love for the process itself, encouraging continuous engagement and exploration.

7. **Affirmation**: I trust my creative instincts and follow them with confidence.

   Trusting oneself leads to genuine and authentic creativity, enhancing the depth and sincerity of one's work.

8. **Affirmation**: I welcome mistakes as opportunities to learn and grow creatively.

   Viewing mistakes as learning opportunities reframes setbacks as valuable experiences that enhance creativity.

9. **Affirmation**: I honor my unique creative vision and express it with pride.

   Valuing one's own unique vision supports individuality and encourages authentic creative expression.

10. **Affirmation**: My creativity enriches my life and those around me.

Recognizing the impact of creativity on oneself and others reinforces the importance and value of creative pursuits.

11. **Affirmation**: I am continuously learning and evolving my creative abilities.

Commitment to continuous growth and learning fuels an ever-evolving creative practice.

12. **Affirmation**: I am patient with my creative process and know that great ideas take time.

Emphasizing patience supports the understanding that creativity is a process, and valuable insights may take time to develop.

13. **Affirmation**: I celebrate my creative successes, whether big or small.

Celebrating all achievements encourages ongoing creative efforts and builds confidence.

14. **Affirmation**: I create a positive space that nurtures my creativity.

Fostering a positive environment supports a conducive space for creativity to flourish.

15. **Affirmation**: I see challenges as creative opportunities waiting to be explored.
Reframing challenges as opportunities encourages inventive problem-solving.

16. **Affirmation**: My creativity is a powerful tool for self-expression and connection.

Recognizing creativity as a means of communication and connection enhances its personal and social relevance.

17. **Affirmation**: I freely experiment with my ideas without fear of judgment.

    Experimentation without fear fosters a space for uninhibited creative exploration.

18. **Affirmation**: I value collaboration and see the creative potential in others.

    Emphasizing collaboration fosters a more dynamic and multifaceted creative process.

19. **Affirmation**: I use my creativity to contribute positively to the world.

    Aligning creativity with purpose gives meaning and direction to one's creative pursuits.

20. **Affirmation**: I maintain a balance between my creative work and rest, knowing both are essential.

    Recognizing the importance of rest and balance ensures a sustainable and healthy creative practice.

21. **Affirmation**: I am a creator, and my work is an extension of myself.

    Embracing oneself as a creator personalizes the creative process and deepens the connection to one's work.

22. **Affirmation**: I approach my creative work with curiosity and a sense of adventure.

    Cultivating a sense of wonder and exploration adds excitement and discovery to the creative process.

🌸 Blooming into Your Best Self: Celebrating Your Journey So Far 🌸

Wow! You've come so far! It's truly remarkable to see how much dedication you've poured into fostering a more positive mindset. Just like a flower that has been nurtured and cared for, you're now in full bloom, radiating beauty, strength, and positivity. As you celebrate this significant milestone in your journey, take a moment to reflect on your growth and appreciate the blossoming new version of yourself.

Imagine if we compared this journey to planting a garden. At the start, you prepared the soil, sowed the seeds of positivity, and began to cultivate a space of growth. With each affirmation, you watered those seeds, ensuring that they had the nourishment they needed to flourish. Today, you stand in a vibrant garden, bursting with color and life, a testament to your hard work and commitment.

Here's a special quote to commemorate this moment:

"The mind is like soil. When nurtured with positive thoughts, it blooms into flowers of peace, joy, and success." - Unknown.

As you look ahead, remember that this garden of positivity is yours to tend, cherish, and enjoy. The next leg of your journey promises even more growth, so keep tending to your mind and soul with the same love and dedication.

Celebrate this milestone by treating yourself to something special. Perhaps a day of relaxation, a favorite meal, or simply some quiet time in a place you love. Remember, this is not just about the destination but the beautiful journey. Here's to the blossoming you! 🌷💐

Onward and upward, dear reader. You're doing amazing! 🐢📚🕊️

1. **Affirmation**: I know that creativity takes courage, and I am brave.

Acknowledging the courage needed for creativity empowers one to take risks and venture into the unknown.

2. **Affirmation**: I see failures as stepping stones in my creative journey.

   Reframing failures as part of the journey fosters resilience and determination.

3. **Affirmation**: I engage with my creativity in ways that bring me fulfillment and joy.

   Aligning creativity with personal fulfillment enhances the satisfaction and meaning derived from creative endeavors.

4. **Affirmation**: I listen to constructive feedback and use it to enhance my creative work.

   Embracing feedback as a valuable resource supports growth and refinement in one's creative practice.

5. **Affirmation**: I am committed to my creative passions and make time for them regularly.

   Demonstrating commitment to creativity ensures consistent practice and nurtures continuous growth.

6. **Affirmation**: I embrace my creative journey with love, knowing it is a true expression of my soul.

   Embracing creativity with love affirms its connection to one's essence and encourages deep and personal engagement.

These affirmations serve to inspire and support anyone looking to delve into their creative abilities, whether you are a seasoned artist or someone just beginning to explore. By weaving these positive affirmations into your daily routine, you can unlock the doors to your creative potential and embark on a fulfilling and transformative journey.

CHAPTER 11:

Inner Strength and Resilience

A lighthouse stands tall amidst the roaring waves and storms. Its light pierces through the darkest nights, providing hope and direction for lost ships. Imagine if we could all be like lighthouses, unwavering in the face of adversities, shining our light, and standing strong no matter the challenge. You might wonder, what powers the lighthouse to remain steadfast? It is its foundation, built deeply into the ground, and its purpose is to guide and save.

So, what's your foundation? What's your inner strength? We all possess an incredible reservoir of resilience and strength within us. Often, it remains untapped, hidden beneath layers of self-doubt, past traumas, and external pressures. Yet, this strength is waiting to be acknowledged and nurtured.

In this chapter, we'll explore affirmations designed to remind you of your inner power and your unyielding spirit. Because just like that lighthouse, you are also built to withstand storms. You have faced challenges before, and you have overcome them. But sometimes, amidst the chaos and noise, we forget our victories and focus on our defeats.

The journey of discovering your inner strength starts with a single affirmation. Let it be the light that guides you in your darkest moments. Allow yourself to be inspired and remember that no matter how turbulent the seas are, you have the power to shine through.

Daily Affirmations

Embrace these affirmations, say them out loud, and believe in them. You are about to embark on a transformative journey that will uncover the lighthouse within you, revealing your true strength and resilience.

Ready to light up your world? Let's begin! 🎇

1. **Affirmation:** I am strong enough to face life's challenges with courage.

   This affirmation reinforces the belief in one's inner strength, providing the confidence to handle any obstacle that may arise.

2. **Affirmation:** I bounce back from setbacks with renewed determination.

   Emphasizing the ability to recover from difficulties, this affirmation fosters a resilient mindset, enabling growth from experiences.

3. **Affirmation:** I trust myself to make the right decisions.

   Trusting oneself in decision-making builds confidence and assures that even in uncertainty, the right path will be found.

4. **Affirmation:** My challenges shape me into a stronger person.

   Viewing challenges as opportunities for growth and strength empowers one to face them with optimism and determination.

5. **Affirmation:** I embrace my fears and learn from them.

   By embracing and learning from fear, this affirmation promotes a courageous approach to life, turning obstacles into learning opportunities.

6. **Affirmation:** I am resilient, and nothing can keep me down.

   This bold statement of resilience encourages a never-give-up attitude, which is essential for pursuing dreams and goals.

7. **Affirmation:** My inner strength is greater than any obstacle.

Reaffirming that inner strength surpasses any challenge; this affirmation empowers readers to face difficulties head-on.

8. **Affirmation:** I learn from my mistakes and grow stronger every day.

   Recognizing mistakes as learning opportunities fosters a growth mindset, leading to personal improvement and strength.

9. **Affirmation:** I am in control of my emotions and respond with wisdom.

   Emotional intelligence is key to resilience; this affirmation encourages thoughtful responses rather than reactive behaviors.

10. **Affirmation:** I am adaptable and thrive in any situation.

    Flexibility and adaptability are essential for resilience. This affirmation nurtures the ability to thrive in various circumstances.

11. **Affirmation:** My courage and determination are unstoppable.

    By believing in unstoppable courage and determination, readers are encouraged to pursue their dreams relentlessly.

12. **Affirmation:** I am confident in my abilities and trust my judgment.

    Building confidence in one's judgment fosters a strong, independent mindset, which is vital for personal growth.

13. **Affirmation:** I face uncertainty with a calm and peaceful mind.

    Facing uncertainty with calmness promotes inner strength and the ability to navigate unknown situations with grace.

14. **Affirmation:** I turn my wounds into wisdom.

    This powerful affirmation teaches that even painful experiences can be transformed into valuable lessons.

15. **Affirmation:** I am grateful for my inner strength and resilience.

Gratitude for inner strength enhances self-awareness and creates a positive cycle of resilience.

16. **Affirmation:** I believe in myself and my ability to succeed.

   Belief in oneself is a cornerstone of inner strength, enabling one to pursue success with confidence.

17. **Affirmation:** I choose to respond to challenges with positivity and grace.

   Choosing a positive response to challenges fosters resilience and shows mastery over life's circumstances.

18. **Affirmation:** I am patient with myself and trust the process of life.

   Patience and trust in life's process promote a balanced and resilient approach to personal development.

19. **Affirmation:** I let go of what I cannot control and focus on what I can.

   Letting go of uncontrollable factors and focusing on actionable steps fosters resilience and a sense of empowerment.

20. **Affirmation:** I am determined to succeed, no matter the obstacles.

   This affirmation instills a relentless pursuit of success, regardless of the hurdles along the way.

21. **Affirmation:** I embrace failure as a stepping stone to success.

   Viewing failure as a stepping stone to success turns setbacks into opportunities, strengthening resilience.

22. **Affirmation:** I surround myself with positive energy and supportive people.

   Building a positive support network reinforces resilience and strength in facing life's challenges.

23. **Affirmation:** I have the power to change my life and overcome any challenge.

    Emphasizing the innate power to change and overcome challenges promotes self-belief and determination.

24. **Affirmation:** I acknowledge my fears but do not let them rule me.

    Acknowledging fears without being ruled by them builds courage and strength to overcome challenges.

25. **Affirmation:** I grow stronger with each experience, whether good or bad.

    Embracing all experiences as opportunities for growth cultivates a resilient mindset, ready to learn and evolve.

26. **Affirmation:** I am a survivor and thrive in adversity.

    Identifying as a survivor who thrives in adversity creates an indomitable spirit, ready to face life head-on.

27. **Affirmation:** I believe in the power of positive thinking and its ability to heal me.

    Faith in the healing power of positivity nurtures inner strength and the ability to recover from emotional wounds.

28. **Affirmation:** I am enough, and my strength is limitless.

    Recognizing oneself as enough and possessing limitless strength fuels self-acceptance, resilience, and empowerment.

The affirmations in this chapter offer a transformative experience, guiding you on a journey towards inner strength and resilience. Each affirmation is thoughtfully crafted to uplift, motivate, and instill a sense of invincibility. Through consistent practice, you can expect to build a fortified mindset, ready to embrace life's challenges with courage and grace. 🚀💪

CHAPTER 12:
Finding Joy in Small Things

Have you ever watched a child lose themselves in the simple joy of watching a butterfly flutter by or laughing at the ripples formed by a stone thrown into a pond? Their pure delight in these fleeting moments is a testament to the immense power of life's tiniest treasures. As we grow older, layers of responsibilities, pressures, and external distractions often overshadow these moments. We become attuned to life's grand events, awaiting the next big achievement or celebration to bring us happiness, often overlooking the countless miniature marvels sprinkled throughout our day.

Yet, it's these small moments that often hold the keys to true and lasting happiness. They act as anchors, grounding us in the present and reminding us that joy is not always a product of grandeur–rather, it's stitched together from countless little stitches of everyday wonders.

"Life is made up of a collection of moments that are not ours to keep. The pain we encounter throughout our days spent on this earth comes from the illusion that some moments can be held onto. Clinging to people and experiences that were never ours in the first place is what causes us to miss out on the beauty of the miracle that is the now. All of this is yours, yet none of it is. How could that be? Look around you. Everything is fleeting." – Rachel Brathen.

As we embark on this chapter, let's rekindle that child-like wonder, that innate ability to find joy in the little things. These affirmations will guide you towards embracing and cherishing life's micro-moments, filling your heart with gratitude, joy, and serenity. By focusing on the little things, you're not minimizing life's grand moments but amplifying the spaces in between, making your entire life one continuous, joy-filled journey.

So, are you ready to dive deep into the world of small wonders? Let's begin this transformative chapter by discovering joy in the places we least expect but need the most. 🏵️🦋❄️

1. **Affirmation:** I find joy in every day, and every day brings me joy.

   This affirmation empowers you to seek happiness in the mundane, transforming ordinary moments into extraordinary joy.

2. **Affirmation:** Simple pleasures fill my life with happiness and contentment.

   Acknowledging the value of simple pleasures allows you to live a fulfilling life without always seeking more.

3. **Affirmation:** I appreciate the beauty in the small details.

   Recognizing the beauty in small details enriches your life and deepens your connection with the world around you.

4. **Affirmation:** Every smile I share brightens my world.

   Sharing a smile is a simple act that can profoundly impact your well-being and the people around you.

5. **Affirmation:** I celebrate the little victories in my life.

   Celebrating small successes fosters a positive outlook and encourages you to strive for more.

6. **Affirmation:** I find joy in the laughter of a child.

The pure and uninhibited joy of a child's laughter can be a powerful reminder to embrace life's simple pleasures.

7. **Affirmation:** The warmth of the sun on my face fills me with happiness.

   Embracing natural sensations like the sun's warmth can connect you to simple yet profound joy.

8. **Affirmation:** I take pleasure in my own solitude.

   Finding joy in solitude helps you understand and appreciate your own company, enhancing self-awareness.

9. **Affirmation:** A kind word or gesture can make my day.

   Small acts of kindness can have a significant impact, highlighting the importance of compassion and empathy.

10. **Affirmation:** I am content with what I have, and I am grateful for it.

    Contentment and gratitude for what you have can nurture a joyful and appreciative heart.

11. **Affirmation:** Nature's beauty brings peace and joy to my soul.

    Connecting with nature and its inherent beauty provides a sense of peace and joy that nourishes the soul.

12. **Affirmation:** I find joy in my hobbies and personal passions.

    Pursuing hobbies and personal passions adds color to life and offers an authentic source of joy.

13. **Affirmation:** My connections with friends and family bring me happiness.

    The joy of connecting with loved ones is a precious source of happiness that reinforces the value of relationships.

14. **Affirmation:** I embrace the joy in simple acts of love and kindness.

Acts of love and kindness, no matter how small, create ripples of joy in your life and the lives of others.

15. **Affirmation:** I find happiness in giving without expecting anything in return.

Selfless giving brings a unique joy that enriches your life and the lives of others.

16. **Affirmation:** I savor the flavors of a good meal.

Taking the time to savor and enjoy food is a simple yet profound way to experience joy.

17. **Affirmation:** I find pleasure in the songs of birds.

Tuning into the simple pleasures like the songs of birds can bring unexpected delight.

18. **Affirmation:** A good book brings joy to my heart.

The joy of getting lost in a good book is a timeless pleasure that nurtures the mind and soul.

19. **Affirmation:** I appreciate the calm of a quiet morning.

Embracing the serenity of a quiet morning offers a pure and simple joy to start your day.

20. **Affirmation:** I enjoy the gentle rain and the freshness it brings.

Appreciating the refreshing aspects of rain reconnects you with nature's simple beauty.

21. **Affirmation:** I take joy in the creativity of others.

Celebrating others' creativity encourages a joyful connection to human ingenuity and expression.

22. **Affirmation:** I embrace the happiness of a warm hug.

    The warmth and connection of a hug can bring simple yet profound happiness to your life.

23. **Affirmation:** I delight in the twinkle of the stars at night.

    Gazing at the stars can evoke a sense of wonder and joy, connecting you to the universe.

24. **Affirmation:** I cherish the joy of a handwritten note from a loved one.

    Personal and heartfelt communication, like a handwritten note, carries a special joy that transcends the ordinary.

25. **Affirmation:** I take pleasure in the success of others.

    Celebrating others' success fosters a sense of community and shared joy, enhancing your positive outlook.

26. **Affirmation:** I find joy in my own personal growth.

    Recognizing and embracing your personal growth offers a unique and empowering source of joy.

27. **Affirmation:** I take time to enjoy the scent of flowers.

    Taking a moment to enjoy simple sensory pleasures like the scent of flowers enriches your daily experience.

28. **Affirmation:** I celebrate life every single day.

    Embracing life in all its fullness and celebrating it daily transforms ordinary existence into an extraordinary journey.

These affirmations encourage you to shift your focus from chasing grand achievements to recognizing and embracing the joy in everyday experiences. By connecting with the simple and often overlooked aspects of life, you are empowered to live a richer, more fulfilling, and happier life. 💥

CHAPTER 13:

Sustaining Positivity

As the ancient Greek philosopher Heraclitus once said, "Change is the only constant in life." While our journey so far has been filled with moments of joy, reflection, and growth, maintaining this newfound positivity in the ever-evolving dance of life is the true challenge.

The Journey So Far: Over the past year, you've dived deep into the wellsprings of your soul, embarking on a transformative journey of self-love, gratitude, confidence, and more. You've not only equipped yourself with the tools to face life's highs and lows but have also cultivated a sanctuary within, where you can always find solace.

As you turned each page and recited each affirmation, a tiny seed of change was planted. And with each passing day, those seeds grew, blossoming into a garden of positivity. This garden is your creation, a testament to your commitment and the potent power of positive affirmations.

But here's the thing about gardens: they need continuous care.

The Challenge Ahead: In this final chapter, we'll explore the art of sustaining the positivity you've worked so hard to cultivate. It's easy to be positive when the sun shines bright, but real growth happens when we learn to dance in the rain, and even find joy in the storm.

Embrace this chapter as the beginning of a new journey, one that's not about discovering positivity but nurturing and sustaining it. This isn't the end; it's the beginning of a lifelong romance with positivity.

Daily Affirmations

Take a deep breath, align with your intentions, and step forward with an open heart. The world needs your light, and this chapter will ensure it never dims. 🦋 🕊️

Are you ready to sustain the vibe, champion the grind, and elevate your life with consistent positivity? Let's dive in! 🚀 📚 🐾

1. **Affirmation:** I embrace positivity as a way of life.
   This affirmation reminds readers that positivity isn't just a temporary phase but a lifelong commitment to a happier existence.
2. **Affirmation:** Every day, I choose joy and contentment.
   By consciously choosing joy, readers reinforce their ability to find happiness in everyday life, even in mundane moments.
3. **Affirmation:** I am in control of my emotions and thoughts.
   This affirmation empowers readers to take charge of their mental and emotional states, enabling them to sustain positivity.
4. **Affirmation:** I spread positivity to others, and it returns to me tenfold.
   Encourages the idea that sharing positivity with others not only enhances their lives but also enriches the individual's life as well.
5. **Affirmation:** My inner peace is unshakeable.
   This affirmation instills a belief in unwavering inner peace, creating a stable foundation for continued positivity.
6. **Affirmation:** I trust the process of life and stay positive throughout.
   Trusting life's journey helps in maintaining a positive attitude, no matter what twists and turns come your way.
7. **Affirmation:** My positivity radiates and inspires others around me.

Recognizing the impact of one's positivity on others creates a sense of purpose and encourages the continued practice of positive thinking.

8. **Affirmation:** I am grateful for my journey and excited for what's next.

   Embracing gratitude for the past and excitement for the future ensures a sustained positive outlook on life.

9. **Affirmation:** I am a beacon of love, hope, and positivity.

   Viewing oneself as a symbol of love and hope reinforces self-worth and encourages continued positive thinking.

10. **Affirmation:** My positive mindset attracts success and abundance.

    This affirmation reinforces the belief that a positive attitude is instrumental in attracting success in all areas of life.

11. **Affirmation:** I am committed to nurturing my positive habits every day.

    Commitment to daily practice ensures that positivity becomes a permanent part of one's lifestyle.

12. **Affirmation:** I turn negatives into positives with ease and grace.

    This affirmation empowers readers to actively transform negative situations into positive experiences.

13. **Affirmation:** My joy is constant, and my positivity never wanes.

    Affirming unwavering joy reinforces the belief that positivity can be maintained regardless of external circumstances.

14. **Affirmation:** My happiness is my priority, and I cultivate it daily.

    Acknowledging the importance of daily cultivation of happiness emphasizes personal responsibility in sustaining positivity.

15. **Affirmation:** I am always learning, growing, and evolving positively.
This affirmation embraces continuous growth and evolution, fostering a lifelong love of learning and personal development.
16. **Affirmation:** I find positive lessons in every experience.
Encourages the habit of seeking valuable lessons even in challenging situations, thus sustaining a positive mindset.
17. **Affirmation:** My positive energy rejuvenates me and those around me.
Recognizing the rejuvenating power of positivity helps readers appreciate its far-reaching impact.
18. **Affirmation:** I am resilient, and my positivity helps me bounce back.
Affirming resilience instills a belief in one's ability to recover from setbacks while maintaining a positive outlook.
19. **Affirmation:** I surround myself with positive influences that nurture my growth.
Encourages readers to consciously choose influences that support their continuous growth and positivity.
20. **Affirmation:** I honor my progress and celebrate my victories, big or small.
Celebrating progress fosters a sense of accomplishment and encourages sustained effort towards maintaining positivity.
21. **Affirmation:** I find joy in the present moment and live positively now.
This affirmation emphasizes the importance of living in the present and finding joy in the current moment.
22. **Affirmation:** My mind is a garden, and I plant only positive seeds.
Symbolizes the nurturing of positive thoughts and the conscious decision to cultivate a positive mental landscape.

23. **Affirmation:** I am content with what I have, yet eager for more growth.

    Balancing contentment with ambition allows for both satisfaction and continual growth in positivity.

24. **Affirmation:** My heart is open to receiving endless positivity and love.

    Encourages an open-hearted approach to life, welcoming positivity and love without reservations.

25. **Affirmation:** I am patient with myself and trust my positive journey.

    Emphasizing patience and trust helps readers to be gentle with themselves as they continue their journey of positivity.

26. **Affirmation:** I transform fear into faith and doubt into determination.

    This powerful affirmation teaches readers to transmute negative emotions into positive driving forces.

27. **Affirmation:** I am the author of my story, and it's a positive one.

    Encourages readers to take charge of their narrative and consciously create a positive life story.

28. **Affirmation:** I end each day with gratitude and begin anew with hope.

    Integrating gratitude and hope into daily rituals ensures the continuity of positivity from one day to the next.

By embracing these affirmations, you are encouraged to make positivity a daily practice, embedding it into your very way of living. This may be the final chapter that concludes your journey within the book, but tomorrow, you finish with one final affirmation. At the conclusion of your year-long journey, you will leave feeling equipped and empowered with the tools you need to continue growing and thriving, with positivity at the core of your existence.

CONCLUSION

Final Powerful Affirmation:

I am in control of my destiny, and every day brings new opportunities for growth and fulfillment.

This affirmation serves as a daily reminder that you hold the reins of your life. It inspires you to seize the day, take charge of your destiny, and open your heart to the endless opportunities that await you.

The journey towards a positive mindset doesn't end with the closing of this book. It's a continuous process, a practice that requires persistence, patience, and belief in oneself. Wake Up with Positivity has been your companion on this transformative path, guiding you through 13 chapters of inspiration and empowerment.

With each affirmation, you've laid the foundation for a life filled with joy, self-love, and accomplishment. These aren't mere words but powerful tools that have the potential to reshape your thoughts, beliefs, and actions.

As you step into each new day, remember to embrace change, face challenges with resilience, and find joy in the smallest things. Cherish the relationships that surround you and nurture your body and mind with healthy habits. Let creativity flow, believe in abundance, and never let go of your inner strength.

Through this journey, you've learned that positivity isn't something to be sought outside; it resides within you. It's your choice, your decision, your action. The affirmations have served as daily nudges, but the real change has come from within you.

Embrace your power. Embrace your potential. Embrace yourself.

Thank you for allowing this book to be a part of your positive transformation. Keep shining, keep believing, and always remember that you are in control of your destiny, and every new day is a fresh opportunity to grow and fulfill your dreams.

May your life be filled with positivity, and may your mornings always Wake Up with Positivity. 📚 🐛

Conclusion: Embracing a New Dawn with Positivity

Every sunrise brings a promise, a chance to reset, to write a new chapter, and to embrace life with renewed energy. As you've journeyed through this book, each affirmation has been a beacon, a guidepost pointing you towards the vast potential within you.

❈ "I am the master of my thoughts, and every day, I choose positivity." ❈

This affirmation isn't just words—it's a proclamation, a statement of your inner strength, resilience, and unwavering belief in your potential. Understand its significance: You hold power to shape your reality, mold your perceptions, and take control of your life's narrative.

Positivity is more than just a mindset; it's a lifestyle, a conscious choice made every day. It's an acknowledgment of challenges and a fierce determination to rise above them. It's embracing each morning with gratitude, hope, and an insatiable hunger to make the most out of every moment.

As you close this book, remember that your journey doesn't end here. Instead, it's just the beginning of a new chapter filled with possibilities, adventures, and breakthroughs. The affirmations you've practiced over the past months are your allies, empowering you to face life's ebb and flow with grace, courage, and a smile.

Daily Affirmations

Doubts and hurdles may arise, but armed with your newfound positive outlook, they become mere stepping stones towards your grander goals. Each affirmation serves as a reminder of your inherent worth, potential, and the boundless opportunities waiting for you.

Carry this book close to your heart, not just as a collection of affirmations but as a testament to your commitment to personal growth and positivity. Open it whenever you need a dose of inspiration or a reminder of your strength.

Remember, every morning is a fresh canvas. How you choose to paint it is entirely up to you. May your colors be bright, your strokes confident, and your masterpiece filled with joy, love, and positivity.

Now, step into the world with your head held high, knowing that with every sunrise, you're presented with a golden opportunity to Wake Up with Positivity. The world awaits your brilliance. Shine on! 🎨 🔒

Made in United States
Troutdale, OR
12/11/2024

26231605R00056